LINKS TO
UNDERSTANDING

LINKS TO UNDERSTANDING

*A Guidebook for
Intentional Professionals
Working with Aging People*

*Includes information on
Gerontology, Thanatology, and
a chapter on Gerotranscendence
with contributions from
Ann Meissner, Ph.D.*

CAROL LEE BRATTER

Beaver's Pond Press

ISBN 10: 1-59298-224-7
ISBN 13: 978-1-59298-224-0

Library of Congress Control Number: 2008922534
Printed in the United States of America
First Printing, February 2008
11 10 09 08 07 6 5 4 3 2 1

Beaver's Pond Press is an imprint of
Beaver's Pond Group
7104 Ohms Lane, Suite 101
Edina, Minnesota, 55439-2129
www.beaverspondpress.com

To Ben Bratter, Jr.,
the love of my life,
with respect
and grateful appreciation.

Contents

Part Five: Appendices

ACKNOWLEDGMENTS

WITH GRATITUDE AND LOVE, I wish to acknowledge the following, (almost) in order of appearance in my life:

Kathleen Gurbin, my mother, a wise, kind and devout woman who navigated the choppy waters of life and taught me how. She keeps me in her prayers to this day, bless her.

Virginia West, my role model and dear friend for over fifty years, who began as a co-worker and became my boss when our firm moved me to Minneapolis all those years ago. Her belief in me, her support, guidance, and wise counsel motivated and inspired me, then and now.

Dr. Justus E. Olson, who was a pioneer in the human potential movement. As an affiliate of National Training Laboratories, "J" originated the Koinonia Human Relations Training program, an outreach ministry, in the Minneapolis area. His teaching and guidance changed my life, and his legacy of honoring the human spirit continues to change the world, one person at a time.

Ann Meissner, Ph.D., an esteemed, innovative educator and Master therapist much-honored by her peers, who has in recent years become a recognized expert on human development. She was instrumental in introducing the ninth stage of adult development, gerotranscendence, after studying the theory with Lars Tornstam, its originator. Down-to-earth, calm and wise, Ann is a cherished and indispensable friend of over forty years who evokes the best in me, and whose healing presence lights my way.

Dr. Aubrey Daniels, a globally respected business consultant who is a pioneer in the development of applied behavioral science in the education and business arenas. His guidance in applying human potential principles for motivation and productivity to the workplace, while maintaining the highest professional standards, has been key to the success of all my business enterprises. I deeply value the wisdom he has brought to my life as well as his continuing friendship.

Mary Kaye Bryant, a true collaborator and the patient and persistent editor of this manuscript—literally its midwife—who has been my treasured personal and business friend for many years. With uncanny perception, with knowledge and skills diligently applied, with honor and integrity, she is the person most responsible for the completion of this work.

Prologue

THIS BOOK PRESENTS TO "the Intentional Professional" the realities of the workplace, integrating our theoretical understanding of gerontological issues with practical applications into the format of a handbook, or guide, to be used by those of us working as counselors, therapists, chaplains, and other human services specialists within the aging community.

My perspective is holistic, interweaving aspects of widely-held concepts of human and spiritual development with elements synthesized from other disciplines. Current research and publications are referenced for clarity and as suggestions for further study. However, the field of gerontology is growing exponentially, and while all of the content is intended to be relevant and helpful, it will not be all-inclusive or the final word on any topic.

The need for such a guidebook became clear to me when I, wanting to prepare myself for specific training in such work, needed a resource to refer to and found none.

Education regarding human behavior and development is available from books and courses almost anywhere. But they are the map, not the territory. What I had to learn by other (often painful) means, such as careful observation and listening in the cracks, were the unspokens, the unwritten rules and unstated values, that operate in every organization and every work situation.

Most of us are fortunate enough to move along the career track with a solid foundation in book learning, a moral compass, a set of values, and a work ethic, which serve us well as far as they go. But what about developing the "soft skills", which are just as essential? These might include being organized, managing your time well, communicating appropriately, resolving conflict, being an effective leader, and the like. (Not to mention negotiating the tricky waters of organizational politics.)

For your own survival, I strongly recommend that you find a role model, and if possible, a mentor, who can teach you what no classroom or book ever could.

And then we come to the most important aspect of our work: how do we put the "care" in career? This means "care-ing" not only for our clients, but also for ourselves.

I believe that to master this concept, our only option is to continue to grow as human beings and as professionals.

When we fully embrace it, the growth process can develop in us a person integrated in body, mind and spirit, one who can evolve to ever-higher levels of knowledge and wisdom. Persons who are out of balance are subject to burnout, to crises of meaning or of purpose.

The Intentional Professional ever seeks wholeness for self and nurtures it in others. For myself, the keys to wholeness came with the study of human relationships and human development.

The work of your world is important; certain professions stress human values as a base, positive intent as a starting point, with equality and mutual respect as a standard. In choosing your mode of service, make the commitment, then do your utmost to give it your best.

My hope is that you, the Reader, will find here information that is helpful, useable, and inspiring. Use what you can and leave the rest, add to this knowledge as you can, and pass it on when you can.

Blessings,

Carol Lee Bratter
Minneapolis, Minnesota, 2008

Note: Sources and quotes attributed in the text by name only are referenced in the Bibliography.

We Are Transmitters

D. H. Lawrence

As we live, we are transmitting life.
And when we fail to transmit life,
Life fails to flow through us.

That is part of the mystery of sex,
It is a flow onwards.
Sexless people transmit nothing.

And if, as we work, we can transmit
Life into our work,
Life, still more life, rushes into us to
Compensate, to be ready
And we ripple with life through the days.

Even if it is making an apple
Dumpling, or a man a stool,
If life goes into the pudding, good is the
Pudding, good is the stool.
Content is woman, with fresh life rippling into her,
Content is the man.

"Give, and it shall be given unto you"
Is still the truth about life.
But giving life is not so easy.
It doesn't mean handing it out to some mean fool,
Or letting the living dead eat you up.
It means kindling the life-quality where it was not,
Even if it's only in the whiteness
Of a washed pocket handkerchief.

(emphasis the Author's)

Introduction

Overview

FOR YOUR REAL-WORLD WORK as a human services provider to today's aging people, the topics covered in this guide will be relevant and useful, addressing the who, what, how and why in the most practical ways. Where applicable, they are grounded in research and/or addressed in contemporary literature.

Some topics are given fuller treatment than others, not as a sign of relative importance, but to bring lesser-known or newer information to your attention. Other important subjects that already have an extensive bibliography, such as death and dying, are included here only briefly.

In Part One, we present the Ideals that we as professionals continue to strive toward, followed in Part Two by the Realities, which require us to know ourselves as well as we know our jobs.

In Parts Three and Four, we discuss some of the Personal and Interpersonal Issues of greatest concern to our clients and their families, those which help and those which hinder them and us in working toward a satisfactory outcome for whatever situation we are facing. The themes of spirituality, forgiveness, and (gero)transcendence recur throughout.

When situational judgment is required on the job, there may be more than one answer. However, when dealing with legal matters, regulations or sensitive materials used by other professionals and institutions, precise information on a timely basis is mandatory.

The pursuit of current information and continuing education in relevant areas will always be part of your work.

Theoretical Bases

The concepts of Logotherapy and Gerotranscendence form the primary theoretical underpinnings throughout the text, and the content, while secular in nature, can be assumed to be rooted in the Judeo-Christian tradition.

Summary of Logotherapy

Logotherapy is a psychotherapeutic approach developed by Victor Frankl following his experiences in Nazi concentration camps during World War II. The word *logos* denotes "meaning" in Greek.

In his seminal book *Man's Search for Meaning*, Frankl concluded that he and others had survived their ordeal by finding meaning and purpose in their suffering. The task of logotherapy, then, is to restore meaning and purpose to the client's life by placing his or her experiences within a larger context, a philosophy in which the individual assumes responsibility for the *quality* of his or her life, as evidenced by the choices made.

Frankl stated that once we acknowledge the certainty of our own mortality, the urge to discover our unique meaning and purpose presents itself. When life is seen as finite, time takes on new importance; and *if* no obstacle prevents it, the process of dying takes on new meaning and purpose as well.

An "obstacle" is created when we remain chained to the traumatic events of our past, inhibiting the discovery of individual purpose and meaning, exacerbating our pain and suffering, and distorting our perception of all other experience. Ultimately, life may seem empty. As he said in an address to Holocaust survivors, Frankl believed that the *failure to forgive* could form such an inhibiting obstacle. The act of forgiveness, then, can be seen as a spiritual response, the choice to transcend.

"We humans can hope to be girded by spiritual resilience so that, when stripped of all else, we can continue to choose how we will respond to our immutable circumstances " (Frankl).

—based on Kimble, et al,
Victor Frankl's Contribution to Spirituality

Summary of Gerotranscendence
In the early 1970's, Professor Lars Tornstam, Ph.D., presented his introduction to transcendence theory, in which he emphasized the developmental aspects of the aging experience.

In essence, Tornstam is saying: near the end of our middle-age life development cycle, we slowly begin to sense a subtle shift in our way of being in the world. This shift is internal: it is effortless, intuitive, an emergence. We no longer view 'getting older' merely as a continuation of the same life we have been living (Carlsson and Wadensten).

We find ourselves instinctively seeking "right relationship" with all things. Without conscious effort, our attention centers on our sense of "being with" our present experience. We are in process, carried forward, entering a *new* life development cycle, which Tornstam named *gerotranscendence*.

My own experience confirms that this transition takes place within us below the conscious level, most often fueled by our need and desire to understand Life. Our new understanding, in turn, triggers a spontaneous life review from our fresh perspective, our new "knowingness". We begin to see things in a different light. At some level, we let go, and let the energy of the universe support our journey.

Priorities are re-ordered, values are reassessed, needs change; fewer 'things' are necessary or of real importance; we become more selective around how, and with whom, we want to spend our time; we allow ourselves to accept that this life's time is finite.

While the givens of physical environment and availability of human interaction are significant to our process, we still have choices. Avoiding the spectre of an arid emotional life and static existence—which fuels diminished mental and physical health—we intentionally choose to continue to grow into "wise elderhood".

Now widely held is Erik Erikson's original eight-stage developmental model, which begins at birth and ends at maturity. Gerotranscendence is being considered by human development specialists as the ninth, or final, stage of development.

Credible data is now available, namely the Swedish Nurses' Study, a field study that supports Tornstam's gerotranscendence theory and its corollaries. (See Chapter 11 for further elaboration.)

Based on this wealth of valuable new information, present-day models of aging and caregiving are being revised, and the new professional guidelines are worth noting. These changes support empowerment of the individual; optimal care for optimal quality of life; emphasis on preservation of personal dignity; and respect for preferences and privacy, including a quiet environment, elective social participation, and time alone.

—based on the work of Lars Tornstam, Ph.D.

Part One: The Ideal

"Life is lived in the tension between the ideal and the real."
—the Author

CHAPTER ONE: The Ideal Professional
Characteristics of the Ideal Professional

CHAPTER TWO: The Ideal System
Characteristics of the Ideal System

CHAPTER THREE: The Ideal Experience
The Optimal State: Flow

CHAPTER FOUR: The Ideal Role
The Professional's Ideal Role
About Ethics

The Ideal Professional

"Learning the art and science of helping others cope with life's challenges is an important calling . . . Learning how to lessen human suffering and increase human competence, even in small margins, is worthy of great effort."

Characteristics of the Ideal Professional

- Highly functional and emotionally healthy, as evidenced by complete self-acceptance, warts and all.

- Motivated to pursue self-development alongside the ability to help others do the same, while maintaining clear boundaries between the personal and the professional.

- Able to integrate personal life experiences as fuel for further growth as well as the basis for a spirit of empathy and reverence for the human condition.

- Able to grasp the ambiguous complexity of human nature and to view human psychology from its many perspectives.

- Clearly rejects over-simplified theories or models for use with clients.

- Deeply confident in the counseling process and in their own skills, yet accepting of limitations which may hinder the ability to serve every client well.

- Therefore cultivates humility, while keeping grandiosity and arrogance at bay.

- Has the drive to achieve mastery yet never the sense of having fully arrived, remaining a voracious learner of broader as well as work-related subjects.

- Has addressed the developmental issue of integration of the inner and outer selves; works in self-awareness mode.

- Able to entertain feedback yet not be personally destabilized by it.

- Excellent at giving of self to others, with the ability to enter deeply into another's inner world, while maintaining a private self.

- Provides an emotionally safe environment for the client yet can firmly challenge when necessary.

- Adept at harnessing the dynamics of empowering others throughout the helping process.

—adapted from material based on a study of master therapists, presented by Len Jennings, Ph.D, et al, at the College of St. Thomas, Minneapolis, MN

(See also Chapters 4, 5, and 6.)

CHAPTER TWO

The Ideal System

Characteristics of the Ideal System

- The ideal system will be open/adaptive (highly stable, highly flexible), vs. closed/rigid (stable but inflexible), or random/chaotic (flexible but unstable).

- There exists the right to certain privacy and independence, plus ownership of tasks and assignments; autonomy rather than dependency is encouraged.

- A balance is achieved between community/organizational and individual needs.

- Its structure includes various responsibilities with corresponding rights.

- Members have the right to make requests and be heard, while the system retains the right to say no.

- A respectful process is in place for solving problems and resolving difficulties.

- There is clear agreement regarding what members are expected to contribute, and what they will receive in return.

- Members know how they will be measured, and how they will be rewarded.
- All of its members' needs will not be met by this system, as is appropriate.

—based on Gestalt Theory, as adapted by
Carol Lee Bratter, founder, for the
Mentor Center, Minneapolis,
Minnesota, 1990

CHAPTER THREE

The Ideal Experience

The Optimal State: Flow

Flow: "The optimal experience, when things are going well, of an almost automatic, effortless and yet highly focused state of higher consciousness."

When we are experiencing Flow:

- We always know what to do next; our goals are clear.
- We know how well we are doing.
- There is a balance between challenges and skills.
- Our concentration is focused on what we are doing.
- We are aware of what is relevant, here and now.
- There is no worry of failure.
- Self-consciousness disappears.
- Our sense of time becomes distorted.
- The activity becomes *autotelic* (Greek for something that is an end in itself).

—from a summary of a talk by Mihaly Csikszentmihalyi, at a Conference on Creativity and Spirit, sponsored by the Foundation for Human Potential

Further, from a synthesis of my own studies, I have found the following to also be true:

- We receive a stream of life energy that connects us to the cosmic web; it moves in and through us back to the source.

- This life energy may be called the uncaused cause; it is the soul or essence of being.

- A set of urges and drives keeps us striving for more.

- No two persons receive the same gifts to the same degree; there are always similarities and differences. We must play the hand we are dealt.

- All aspects of our involvements, our passions, create dynamic forces of their own.

- *We are accountable for how we use the powers we are given.*

- We are responsible for our own difficulties; it is our job to make our lives work.

- The life force is dynamic; the movement is cyclical, elliptical, evolving to higher and higher levels of development.

- Life spirit is enhanced and strengthened by dealing with obstacles, which creates spiritual resilience.

- Resolving problems, in whatever form, from whatever source, frees up our life energy for investment in spiritual intention.

- Higher levels of awareness are possible if we can transcend our experiences, achieving Flow.

CHAPTER FOUR

The Ideal Role

The Professional's Ideal Role

How is the role of The Intentional Professional changing with the increasing size of the aging population? Major advances in the care and service fields are requiring us to review who we are, what we do, and where we stand on modern-day ethical questions.

The impact is both personal and professional. Recent changes in health care reform and legislation, evolving technology, bio-medical advances, and the budget-based consolidation of social services and community systems require us to rethink and review prior standards, practices, values, and beliefs. We must revalidate our professional identity to know where we stand.

Within the gerontological field, there is heavy emphasis on appropriate action, protection, and privacy regarding vulnerable adults in the aging population. This requires us to be well-informed about and familiar with documentation, compliance, security, and privacy regulations. Further, we must recognize the continuing presence of *ageism* (a form of discrimination) as a major contaminant in the services delivery system.

Professional practice with our older clientele is becoming increasingly complex, and in the future will be more visible in the community: we may function as a linking factor between diverse groups; we may be required to organize a care plan (casework) while working with an interdisciplinary care team; or work with the client's family. We must be knowledgeable and current in the field of gerontology.

Because our effectiveness must bridge a range of populations in various ethnic backgrounds, cultures, denominations of faith, etc., we need to be prepared. And we must be clear about our own personal and professional stance as it relates to emerging ethical issues and social concerns. Thus, continuing education in family therapy methods and counseling theory is strongly recommended for practitioners in the field, who today are also required to acquire knowledge of human development issues— especially of *gerotranscendence* (quality of life)—and end-of-life tasks (death and dying).

About Ethics

Over the past twenty years, we humans have been promised that we can be ageless and nearly immortal: there will be cures for dread diseases, a full array of human replacement organs, and an abundance of improved food for all – as illustrated by a survey of today's bioethical issues:

- The human genome project; genetic engineering of plants, animals, humans
- Cloning – of plants, animals, humans

- Reproductive technology; surrogacy; abortion
- Gene banks; organ transplantation; cryopreservation; euthanasia.

> *"It appears that our research is advancing at such a pace that our ethical understanding of its consequences is unable to keep pace with the moral outcome of our actions".*
>
> —from Matthew Eppinette, Center for Bioethics and Human Dignity, Article, 2004, Richard Kew, *Brave New Church: What the Future Holds*, 2001, and Richard C. Eyer, *Holy People, Holy Lives*, 2000

Our rights and privileges as moral and ethical persons confer on us the responsibility to stay well-informed on these present-day issues, which may even affect us personally, or at times when we feel professionally vulnerable. But science's outpacing of ethics has placed a moral burden on society, which expects us to step in and serve as its conscience in some way or another.

Therefore, as professionals, we must be ready to respond. Over-valuing choices that are practically or emotionally satisfying is a danger: wisdom demands that we prepare ourselves with a carefully reasoned response, reinforcing our commitment to the highest good.

Part Two: The Reality

CHAPTER FIVE

Knowing Your Self

"Live in the now; be present to experience."

—Eckhart Tolle

"Stay aware of experience, but do not allow it to define you. You have *an experience—you are not formed completely by this; you can choose how you define yourself."*

—from Gestalt Theory

"The individual does tend to develop in terms of the sum of their experience. However, it must be perceived, received, and interpreted accurately and then consciously integrated after thoughtful review. To make this process valuable, you must choose a value freely (informed decisions), choose from alternatives, and choose thoughtfully and reflectively."

—Viktor Frankl

Knowing Your Self and Making Choices

In your practice with aging people, you will have many choices to make in terms of your client, the particulars of your client's case, and your professional accountability.

You will be choosing how to respond, what skills to bring to bear, which resources to call upon. Having examined the continuum of your responses to life experiences, your roles and relationships, do you know yourself well enough to now choose your course "thoughtfully and reflectively", as Frankl suggests?

Are you well-informed enough to address this situation? What good can you do? What harm? "Pain [in some form] will be present; learn to recognize it, and create no more." (Tolle). Exactly whom will you be helping? If the client or family is difficult, even threatening, can you forgive and transcend? (The offender/s may act intentionally or unintentionally; the recipient decides whether or not to be the 'victim'.)

The spiritual law of natural consequences will prevail: everything you do and everything you do not do will have consequences. Some consequences may reveal themselves only over time, and possibly not even become known to you. Can you tolerate the implications?

Caring for Your Self and Meditation

"Prolonged contact is painful. Strategic withdrawal is essential to health."
　　　　—from Gestalt Theory, the Awareness Cycle

Periods of quiet, of meditative or contemplative silence, are replenishing for the spirit and may produce fresh awareness and perspective.

All forms of meditation are beneficial; most forms recognize the highest level of consciousness as "enlightenment"; some are described as "listening"—for your ultimate source's wisdom and for aligning your will to the highest good. Over time, an individual may become skillful and develop the ability to intuitively 'know' things.

At first, we engage "beginner's mind": we empty the mind, quiet the mind, and meditate; we prepare to live fully in the present moment with the purest perspective, the highest level of consciousness we are capable of.

If, through meditation or prayer and practicing discernment, we can become ever more fully awake and aware, at ever-increasing levels of consciousness, we can eventually move beyond the material plane toward achieving the ideal stage known as "transcendence".

We thus grow toward personal and professional congruence through the process of integrating the inner with the outer self: an authentic whole self emerges. When we are congruent, we can offer our best selves, fully functioning master professionals, as laborers in the field. Explore the many available resources on the traditions and forms of meditation, until you find one that suits your nature and lifestyle; then use it.

The Use and Abuse of Personal Power

"An effective human being will meet responsibilities, appropriately acknowledge the duties, rights, and privileges of freedom, and function at the highest level of human and moral development they are capable of at any given time, as governed by the best moral and ethical principles they can exercise."

—Lawrence Kohlberg

We are accountable for how we use the powers we are given. These gifts of our human existence may not be used to rob others of their freedoms. The wrong use of power, in its many guises, depletes the spirit, causes toxic emotions, and in its extreme form, promotes evil in the world, as exemplified by Hitler and Stalin.

The converse is also true: the right use of power in and of itself has a transformative effect. Examples abound, as exemplified by the lives of Christ, Gandhi and Mandela. The right use of power over time develops in us "the best moral and ethical principles", transpersonal qualities spiritually inspired. Through practice, it facilitates an enlightened perspective, which may lead us to the state known as gerotranscendence.

The Right Use of Power

The right use of power is highly personal and highly situational. Case by case, we must act to prevent harm and to cause good, practicing discernment and developing the courage to act for positive change.

Modeling civility, not picking up the other end of the rope in a power struggle, and supporting the empowerment of others are powerful acts in interpersonal relationships, as is seeking to equalize unequal relationships rather than exercising any advantage.

Some risks are necessary, but preserving our personal safety in a dangerous situation is paramount; optimally, it can be done without harming or abandoning another in the process. We avoid taking sides, supporting the expression of all points of view. We also avoid taking unnecessary risks, "fixing" people, and making decisions for them (even if we think we know the "right" answer).

It is more respectful to witness the process of others and affirm their ability to make decisions, act for, and ask for what they need and want. In most cases, people are not as fragile as we might think.

Be aware that clients may inadvertently project their own power issues onto you, the nurturing parent figure. Silence, not serving as witness to conflict among others, or removing yourself tactfully are all powerful means of disengaging.

Know that your personal power can be rendered ineffective: if you do *not* use it, you may lose it; you can be conned by a needy person into giving it away to them; or it can be leached away when your ethical values are known and used against you. Beware of manipulators and hidden agendas.

The right use of power is exemplified by the actions of those public figures who have served as our role models:

- Civil disobedience
- Passive resistance
- Campaigning for human equality/rights
- Being unwilling or refusing to engage in a conflict
- Surrendering
- Negotiating peaceful solutions.

The Abuse of Power
The serious abuse of power results in scarring of the human soul; these "Sins of the Spirit" include:

- Causing others to suffer: No one has the right to harm the spirit of another. When we understand that we are all connected spiritually and that what we do to another we do to ourselves, we will change our behavior.

- Ignoring: We collude with the behavior we deplore through silence, indifference, and inaction. We change by being authentic, by speaking up for our values.

- Imbalance and injustice: We restore balance when we optimize all aspects of a system rather than favoring one over another. We seek justice for all when we honor all souls as equals.

- Severing relations: We can do damage by treating relationships as insignificant. We evolve when we commit to working with others through changes and transitions in our relationships.

- Dualism: *Either/or* thinking locks us into reactive and repetitive choices. *Both/and* thinking opens us to new opportunities, new possibilities.

- Lack of passion: A mechanical view of life restricts energy. Living on purpose engenders passion.

—Matthew Fox

CHAPTER SIX

Knowing Your Work

Case Management

The definition of case management:
Case management is primarily the process of linking clients with needed services by locating and coordinating essential community resources and then, where feasible, facilitating informed client decisions.

Specific characteristics of case management:

- Individualized to the unique needs of each client
- Based on a holistic perspective that views all pertinent aspects of the individual, situation and environment
- Focuses on client values and preferences
- Involves the client in identifying and solving problems
- Encourages autonomy; enhances self-care and self-determination
- Aims to provide continuity of appropriate care through optimal choices
- Employs a wide range of services and resources from both formal and informal systems.

The process of case management:

- Case finding: outreach, eligibility determination, intake
- Assessment: current status/problem identification
- Care planning: develop plan addressing needs
- Coordination: arrange delivery
- Follow-up: monitor clients/services
- Reassessment: reevaluation
- Case closure: discharge.

—Source: *Dictionary of Pastoral Care*, pp. 147-148

A note of caution: Well-intended families or caregivers of clients who are ill or disabled can inadvertently cause disenfranchisement of a loved one. For instance: such clients are at high risk when moved from place to place; if they are unable to see, hear or communicate, personal items may be lost, or new medicines introduced without their awareness. The task of answering questions, of monitoring and following up this transition process, may fall to the case manager.

While all case management seeks to coordinate services, most programs are closely tied to their funding sources, which often define the model to be used, the target population, eligibility factors, tools of measurement, etc. It may be the case manager's initial task to learn the specific parameters of each program or model.

Compliance, Accountability, Documentation

The highest professional standards must be practiced consistently. Institutions are culpable, and practitioners are susceptible to errors and omissions. Human beings in need and receiving care are vulnerable, and most are not at their best in times of crisis.

We need to become students of the laws, regulations, policies and guiding principles of our respective professions, including your state's Privacy Act with regard to the sharing of information.

We should keep a dated, client-specific activity log, and keep it current. Case completion and follow-through on a timely basis are vital. We must deal in fact, not interpretations or assumptions, and report mistakes immediately in order to make remedies possible.

In some cases a Durable Power of Attorney is in place, so a counselor or chaplain acting as case manager must validate its existence. In all cases, the client must sign any written Request for Information from a third party, such as a physician, and the service provider must have a signed Permission for Disclosure from the client.

Confidentiality and discretion are mandatory.

(See also Appendix A, Potential Legal Issues for Senior Citizens.)

Some currently accepted standard professional practices include:

- Connecting with your client and team members appropriately
- Monitoring on-site events and behavior

- Maintaining charting, logging, and other reporting systems on a timely basis, as required by the program and by regulatory agencies

- Clarifying your roles and duties regarding the division of labor, respecting professional boundaries: know who does what; get clear on whom to contact and when as well as whom to ask for help (ask!); be aware that multiple crises may require extra professional help

- In the event that problems or conflicts of interest arise, or disharmony within your team occurs, remembering who is the client; contact your "point" person; be willing to be reassigned if necessary.

The Process of Completion

Individual: In one sense, the concept of the "completion" of any issue is a paradox. The various stages of human development evoke the emergence of theme issues, which may present repeatedly throughout the journey.

Client: Within the stated parameters for working with the client, there tend to be indicators that this piece of work, for this period of time, is ready to be concluded. Mutual understanding and a joint decision, with the client or with the survivors, to "end here" and "end now" is essential. Then the appropriate paperwork, notifications, etc., can be processed.

System: As an integral part of a system, the completion process necessitates proper communication, leaving responsibly, a clean ending, letting go, but not precluding the possibility of return if warranted.

The Relationships per se: Professionals note well: recognize that if you should work with this team, client, or family again, you will be forming a new relationship. Any casual contact in the interim must still honor boundaries and confidentiality.

Professional Relationships: Completion tends to follow certain patterns: after the closing comes the honoring of relationships along with the good-byes. Networking, with its own etiquette, may come into play. Continued discretion is required.

Community: The completed case may contribute documented evidence of progress, for example, toward improved quality of life, engendering new laws, environmental changes, new leadership and so forth, as sponsored by any number of proactive organizations.

End of Life Tasks: When death is imminent, end-of-life tasks should be addressed in a cooperative mode, supporting a more peaceful passing, comforting loved ones as they let go, and facilitating the grief process. As a gerontological care provider, your role is to witness, guide, support and comfort during this *final* "process of completion".

CHAPTER SEVEN

Perspectives on the Issues

Gerontology

In 1903, *gerontology* was proposed by M. Elie Metchnikoff as both a new term and a new science; his prediction that its study would bring about great modifications in the course of the last period of life triggered new research in other fields as well. Contemporary gerontology includes the following:

1) scientific study of the processes associated with aging;
2) scientific study of mature and aged adult populations;
3) studies from the perspective of the humanities (history, philosophy and literature); and
4) application of the knowledge gained for the benefit of older adults.

The distinction between studies of processes and of populations is particularly salient: determining the characteristics (biological, psychological and social) of mature adults does not necessarily address questions about the processes inherent in aging *per se*.

—citing Metchnikoff, *Encyclopedia of Aging*, pp. 416-417

Note: *gerontology* should not be confused with *geriatrics*, the branch of medicine that deals with medical issues and diseases in the aging population. The base word, *geron,* comes from the Greek for "old man".

Ageism

"Western civilization treats the elderly with a kind of benign contempt."

—Betty Friedan, speaking at
Hamline University, 1995

Ageism is any form of prejudice based on age; in some cases, it is discrimination.

Gerontophobia is an irrational fear of aging, a negative perception of what it means to grow old, or a prejudice against the aging population, based on disempowering cultural stereotypes (Schachter-Shalomi).

Our culture, young and old alike, has come to think of "old age" as beginning at year sixty-five and having these characteristics:

- Having trouble thinking, remembering, and learning
- Being unhappy, fearful, and depressed
- Being incapable of change, rigid
- Feeling isolated, alone, disconnected from family and friends
- Becoming relatively unproductive in society

- Feeling sick, debilitated
- Being sexless.

Society perpetuates ageism through these common myths (taken from a lecture by Catherine Johnson, administrator of Roitenberg Family Assisted Living Residence):

- Viewing aging as an inevitable process of decline
- Media images with emphasis on youth culture as more valuable
- Corporate cultural values favoring younger employees
- Internalized negative images of the aging population
- Aging as "disease" vs. natural process.

For the most part, the negative stereotyping of ageism does not hold true in today's world. While there may be a loss in thinking speed and memory due to normal processes, the aging population in the new millennium is painting a new picture:

- Mental disorder is *not* inevitable
- Change can enhance the quality of life
- The aging population is highly diverse—a substantial number work for pay, volunteer, or provide caregiving
- Should a situation suggest that such help is needed, older adults can benefit from psychotherapy
- Older persons who continue sexual, romantic relationships report that these often become deeper, fuller, and more satisfying.

In the past, aging was seen as a regressive process. We can now view aging as a developmental process. New research and information from Lars Tornstam, Ph.D. calls aging possibly the ninth stage of development (after Erikson), *gerotranscendence*. He states that our experience does not define who we are, i.e., being "older" does not make us "elderly"; rather, it is our reaction to aging and its consequences that forms us. He believes that our developmental task in elderhood is to rise above our painful experiences and learn from them, achieve a state of ultimate maturity, and in the process, transcend aging itself.

My Story

Even though my studies and coaching practice have focused on the present-day agingcommunity, I must confess: my experience with my own aging process has been an unwelcome surprise to me. Specifically, as a member of the "silent generation" (pre-boomer), I want to disguise the unavoidable signs I have experienced that are common to many people my age: uninvited weight gain, dimming vision, fading skin and hair color, losing hair (and growing it where none used to be). I recognize that I have reacted with my own brand of "ageism" to aging cohorts, with thoughts like, "I hope I don't walk/talk/look like *that!*" Part of me wants to dis-identify from people I love because I do not want to be put in that category: showing my age.

On the inside, I feel the same as I always have; but on the outside, whether I want it to or not, everything is changing. People have started to treat me differently; they are overly helpful, speak loudly, use simplified language, and are frequently condescending or demeaning. I have had to make a conscious effort to maintain my self-confidence.

Finally, to avoid becoming overwhelmed, defeated or worse, depressed, about the inevitable, I have found that *skill* and *mastery* are a wonderful way to be in the world, at any age. Brain researchers are proving that brain cells can be regenerated after all; new software is being developed that proves certain brain cells can be retrained. I therefore strongly encourage lifelong learning for everyone, including a conscious effort to maintain what is now called "brain fitness" (see Appendix C. Brain Fitness/Research).

Related Issues for the Aging Person to Address

The Meaning of Aging. For people as they grow older, the issue of meaning becomes urgent. They may ask questions such as: "What has been the meaning of living this long?" "Is growing old worth working my whole life to attain?" "Is what I have done or not done been or not been enough to sustain me in my last years?" Each person's answers will be theirs alone.

The Legacy of Aging. The 'abundance' of my legacy seems to reflect my contributions toward it; the 'value' of my legacy will be measured by those who benefit from it; the 'ultimate worth' of my legacy will be measured by whether it is replenished and/or augmented over time. So what legacy do I wish to leave?

—from Frederic M. Hudson, the Hudson Institute

The Dilemma of Aging. Nobody knows anything for sure.
—from Ann Meissner, Ph.D.

Quality-of-Life Issues of Aging. There will be a hunger for community. Accepting the need to become less independent gracefully will be a transformative experience. My attachments and detachments will change. I will be either a participant or an observer, and this point of view will affect my daily activities. My emotional needs will increase, and as I seek closer connection, I will grow spiritually. I may express unconditional love. I can surrender spiritually by giving up 'control' over my life. Prayer in its many forms may become central to my life.
—from Susan McFadden, Professor,
University of Wisconsin

Misfortunes are reframed as blessings. Gratitude emerges for graces received.
—from Richard Emmunds

The issue of forgiveness, with its many facets, becomes paramount.
—the Author

The Ultimate Issue of Aging: Dying. Every one of us, client and professional alike, faces the same task: coming to terms with our own mortality, which, in our technology-oriented culture, is often seen as some sort of 'cosmic error' that can be fixed. But as Rabbi Schachter-Shalomi writes further, the more we can embrace the sacred, transcendent nature of death as once experienced by our ancestors, the more our fears and anxieties can transform into feelings of awe and appreciation for life.

Kimble, et al, posit the following as the paradoxes of death:

- While death may be universal for all, we each believe our own death to be unique.

- Death is the end, yet it permeates all of life.

- We know death intellectually, but experientially have difficulty believing it. Sub-consciously, every one of us is convinced of our own immortality (after Freud).

- All humans, in all cultures, are called to deal with the issues of time vs. aging vs. mortality.

- Death is a biological event and at the same time a spiritual phenomenon.

—from *Aging, Spirituality and Religion*, Kimble, et al

Thanatology

Thanatology *is the scientific study of life, with death left in. It encompasses thoughts, values, attitudes, behaviors, relationships, and bio-medical states, as these manifestations of life intersect with the processes of death.* [The word *thanatos* is from the Greek for "death instinct".]

—as defined in *The Encyclopedia of Aging*, p. 931

The field of thanatology, still expanding, has grown to include all aspects of subjects such as death and dying, including grieving and loss; hospital and hospice treatments, including alternative medicines and therapies;

and mortuary practices and their effects—in short, the entire spectrum of the death experience. The implications and applications of its findings have impacted all related disciplines in science and the humanities, and like gerontology, have engendered new disciplines.

—citing Metchnikoff, *The Encyclopedia of Aging*, pp. 413-417

Especially effective is thanatology's holistic, unbiased worldview of the value and validity of the funereal and burial practices of multiple ethnic groups, cultures, denominations, and spiritual and wisdom traditions. The need of survivors for meaningful rituals, and for the counsel of trained professionals, was never more apparent than following the tragedies of September 11, 2001. Thanatology's integrative approach is beneficial to practitioners who must deal with such matters with clients, applying, for example, the principles of the grieving process, bringing comfort and healing by helping the survivors with troublesome issues of the mind, body or spirit.

CHAPTER EIGHT

Spirituality

*As used herein, **spirituality** "refers to a lived experience that includes attitudes, beliefs and practices that animate (give spirit to) people's lives".*
—Ramsey & Blieszner

"Spirituality is universal; religion is cultural."
"Religion tends to become the container for spirituality."
—from remarks by Ann Meissner, Ph.D.

As professionals working with clients from all backgrounds, we need to understand the difference between what *they* may perceive, and name, as being "spiritual" and being "religious". In addition, in order to avoid contaminating the helping process, we must be clear about our own views of these concepts.

"Spirituality" and "religiosity", though often mis-identified each as the other, are not the same thing. Each can exist without the other; yet they can and do co-exist within an individual, and may have characteristics in common.

Human spirituality, uniquely individual, expresses itself in limitless numbers of ways. Yet there is nothing inherently spiritual about practicing a certain religion or belonging to a particular group, be it an ashram or a church congregation.

Spirituality is not a feeling; it is an experience, a response. But reporting certain types of 'significant' experiences (emotions, thoughts, sensations) does not necessarily qualify them as being spiritual.

While spirituality and "flow" are not the same thing (Thompson), spirituality may provide the setting for flow, and certain states of flow may be described as religious or transcendent (Csikszentmihalyi). (See also Chapter 3. The Optimal State: Flow.)

As Schachter-Shalomi posits, sectarian religions today generally provide followers with externally-imposed beliefs, practices and rituals, which (ironically) give the comfort of social belonging and at the same time tend to separate some groups of believers from others. Their approach tends to rely heavily on the intellectual and verbalized aspects of doctrine, such as sermons and prayer, which perfectly fulfill what their followers expect of them.

Spirituality, on the other hand, implies a self-directed approach, a search for one's own inner truth. Seekers are willing to open themselves to the implications of their inquiry. Developing contemplative, meditative and/or intuitive skills leads to new insights and realizations—one of which may be that all people, in their own way and regardless of affiliation, are united in the same quest, for connection with Spirit.

CHAPTER NINE

Intimacy and Isolation

Intimacy

"The word intimate *is derived from the Latin "intimus," designating the person or thing that is innermost, most familiar or internal. In relationship, it marks one most closely associated or acquainted".*
—*Dictionary of Pastoral Care and Counseling*

The professional human services provider is in the paradoxical position of dealing with the most personal matters of a client's life while maintaining a certain detachment, allowed to see into an intimate space without actually walking into or invading that space. Boundaries are established, identifying the most comfortable balance between closeness and distance; psychological-territory needs and threat-tolerance levels are respected.

While most people think of "intimate" as referring only to close physical relationships, there are actually seven planes of *psychological intimacy* on which we may connect:

- Recreational (pastime, hobby)
- Work- or crisis-related
- Intellectual

- Aesthetic
- Emotional
- Physical
- Spiritual

In healthy psychological intimacy:
- *Contact* occurs when individuals' boundaries meet.
- *Connection* is created as an exchange of energy takes place.
- *Trust* is built along with deepening levels of intimacy.

In any ongoing relationship, like that between counselor and client, psychological intimacy is developed according to each person's needs and tolerances. As deeper levels of intimacy are reached, greater emotional stamina is required to sustain the relationship. Being able to nurture several levels of intimacy creates a powerful, positive energy that feeds spiritual connection with the others in our lives, be they our clients, family, friends, or peers.

Isolation

To *isolate* is defined by Webster's as *"to place apart, to separate from all others"*; a synonym for isolation is *loneliness*. Isolation, then, could be seen as the opposite of, or lack of, intimacy.

It is possible to be yet not feel isolated, as when living alone, i.e., *physical* isolation. It is just as possible to feel isolated while living with others, i.e., *psychological* isolation. A person may experience either or both types.

Older persons who live alone or in institutional settings often feel lonely, depressed, even alienated from their peers, family and friends, especially if they are ill or disabled. Their lives may have been punctuated by a series of losses. They may be harboring an amorphous, unfocused anger—an accumulation of griefs, disappointments, frustrations, old resentments—which may be unleashed when triggered by any negative experience, often inappropriately and out of proportion to current events. Chronically "crabby" people have difficulty making contact, establishing connections, and maintaining functional relationships. This lack of intimacy and social support may contribute to their decline, and vice-versa.

Even healthy older people may find themselves less and less willing to run the risk of self-disclosure required by social interaction, may be less and less inclined to place trust and confidence in individuals and in systems, and may welcome, by choice, a kind of relief in isolation.

However, whether other-imposed or self-imposed, any form of isolation taken to the extreme can be destructive. And the antidote is healthy psychological intimacy.

(*The Yalom Reader*, originated in 1931 by Irvin D. Yalom, M.D., and edited by his son Ben Yalom in 1998, offers an excellent perspective on isolation as an issue for the aging population.)

CHAPTER TEN

Forgiveness

Definition

To *forgive* is defined by Webster's as: *1. To give up claim to compensation, recompense, or retaliation from an offender; to pardon. 2. To give up resentment.*

Forgiveness is an *attitude* of the spirit, a *decision* of the mind and heart, and a *process* that unfolds once the attitude is achieved and the decision is made.

Forgiveness—*of the self or of others*—must be recognized by an individual as a necessary, intentional act of free will; it may be evoked, must be genuine, and is not valid if forced.

Lack of forgiveness is poison for the human spirit.

Guiding Principles in the Counseling Relationship

As professionals, we respect general guiding principles. The following are invoked when working with clients on forgiveness issues:

- Forgiveness is a balance between justice and mercy,

and both parts must be addressed. (Is it just, *and* is it merciful?) Forgiving consists of problem-solving toward a moral, ethical decision, a decision that involves self as well as other(s).

- Forgiveness is a decision to not punish anyone—self or other—for a real or perceived injustice. This decision is a conscious act of will (right use of personal power). Though we may not believe or agree that an injustice has been done, we must remain aware that the perception of injustice is no less painful for the sufferer. Explore and identify the perceived offense within the person's own ethical system.

- Forgiveness is also action taken on the basis of that decision, and the emotional relief and freeing of energy that follows. Such right action will promote:
  —Emotional and physical health
  —Warmer relationships with other people
  —Self-esteem
  —Freeing up energy to invest in working toward justice.

- Forgiveness is an interpersonal issue. Caution to practitioners: there is danger in assuming that we know what the offense was. There may be more to be known; look for the germ of truth; expect resistance and remain nonjudgmental.

- Forgiving is not necessarily refusing to lay blame. Blame can have a variety of meanings:
  —Accurate identification of someone having offended by avoiding responsibility

—Avoidance of facing one's own responsibility for
(participation in) an offense

—Judging on moral or ethical grounds.

The Process

The *process* of forgiveness includes the concept that to
forgive is first to "accuse". The steps in this process are to:

- *Identify* that the discomfort comes from a real or
  perceived offense.

- *Validate* the feelings of the offended; allow the person
  to ventilate (once expressed, feelings can change). It is
  not necessary for us to agree with the subject in order
  to listen to and learn what the person is experiencing.

- *Focus* on thoughtful problem solving. Delay immediate
  action in order to counteract possible retaliation, self-
  blame, shame, withdrawing, gossip, undermining
  tactics, or other destructive behaviors. They only
  make everyone involved feel worse.

- *Counsel caution.* Action decisions should come at the
  very end of the process. Beware of 'pat' formulas and
  recipes. Minimize a chaotic approach and bring order
  to the process, keeping in mind the desired outcome.

- *Work together* on a decision to act or to refrain from
  acting prematurely. This step empowers an individual
  through the ability to choose: right action; right
  intention, timing and context; harmony with one's
  own cultural and ethnic identity; and behaviors in
  keeping with one's own belief system, morals and
  values.

- *Allow time* for the client to process what is happening. Just witness and affirm—do not direct—but do set appropriate boundaries as needed. Take nothing personally.

  —from a Lecture at Colonial Church of Edina by Mona Gustafson, Ph.D., of the Adler Institute, 1999

Categories of Forgiveness

There is increased interest in forgiveness as a topic of focus since the attacks on the World Trade Center and Pentagon in 2001. Consequently, new literature and data are being released even as this manuscript is being published, offering differing perspectives from a variety of disciplines.

In my research, I was able to uncover these main categories of forgiveness (you may know more):

1. Individual/personal forgiveness
2. Forgiveness of self
3. Collective/community forgiveness
4. Forgiving the unforgivable.

(Seeking forgiveness from others requires a different dynamic.)

I will briefly describe and illustrate these as follows

1. A. The Stanford University Forgiveness Project, published as *Forgive for Good*, by Fred Luskin, Ph.D.
   B. The book *Forgiving the Devil*, by Terry Hargrave, Ph.D.
2. The book *Dare to Forgive*, by Edward M. Hallowell, M.D.
3. The Truth and Reconciliation Council (Apartheid Amnesty)

4. A. The Story of Bud Welch (Murder Victims'
   Families for Reconciliation)
   B. The Innocence Project (legal exoneration).

*1A. Individual/Personal Forgiveness: The Forgiveness
Project, Stanford University Department of Disease
Prevention and Health, 1999.*
The stated goals of this classroom study were to:

- Build good skills to manage forgiveness and deal with
  an offense

- Understand how grievances affect physical and
  mental health

- Learn how to raise the threshold by which offense is
  taken.

During the study, it became clear that forgiveness is *not*:

- Condemning unkindness

- Forgetting that something painful happened or
  excusing poor behavior

- 'Other-worldly' or a 'religious' experience

- Minimizing or denying what you want, or giving up
  your feelings.

—from Fred Luskin, Ph.D., Director
of the Forgiveness Project

The findings of the study included:

- Forgiveness training can be effective
- The skill of forgiving can be learned and practiced

- A means of engendering forgiveness is often lacking in our culture
- Forgiveness of self and others may emerge as a painful, end-of-life lesson
- All major religions and wisdoms extol the value of forgiveness
- Physical and emotional problems result if the anger and blame of unreconciled grievances are allowed to persist
- Forgiveness can be thought of as a transforming experience—from negative to positive.

Findings indicate that it is yet to be understood how gender affects willingness to forgive, and whether forgiveness training can be conducted on a larger scale, i.e., at the community level.

> —Carl E. Thorsen, Ph.D., principal investigator

1B. Individual/Personal Forgiveness: Forgiving the Devil, Coming to Terms with Damaged Relationships, *by Terry Hargrave, Ph.D., 2007.*
A more recent presentation of all aspects of forgiveness within relationships, especially families, this book is a model of conciseness and clarity. It is intended for lay persons as well as therapists.

Hargrave's thesis rests on the idea that the origins of all pain in relationships are violations of love and/or of trust. He maintains that the work of forgiveness—to address those violations and heal the damage—can be divided into two broad categories, each appropriate for different situations and at different times: salvage, via insight and understanding; and restoration, via giving the opportunity for compensation, and if possible, overt forgiving. The former method can help us to heal ourselves, the latter to heal our relationships. With compassion for all concerned and meaningful examples, Hargrave lays out a step-by-step process for dealing with each of these elements.

2. Forgiveness of Self: Dare to Forgive, *by Edward M. Hallowell, M.D., 2004.*

Hallowell says it eloquently:

> "Love allows us to forgive ourselves more often than not . . . The hard part is finding that love. Often that love does not—or will not in spite of our best efforts—arise from within us. So then it must come from the outside: from a friend, a lover, perhaps a pet, or from that force some call God.

> "Forgiving yourself all by yourself is tough. I have seen people spend decades suffering from their own self-contempt, unable to find forgiveness from themselves. They never looked outside themselves because they didn't dare; they believed that others would scorn them even more than they scorned themselves. But they were never able to forgive themselves on their own, because forgiveness is usually an interactive process. When you need forgiveness for yourself, you need someone or something outside of yourself to interact with to make it possible.

"If you choose the right kind of person, you will find that that person can help you simply by listening. Most of the time, your judgment of yourself is more severe than anyone else's. When you speak it out and let someone else hear, you start to feel better. The process of self-forgiveness can be slow, but it will begin once you connect with another person.

"The reason others can help you in this way is simple. We're all in the same boat, just not at the same time. We all need to be forgiven at some time or another . . ." Choose someone you trust and who you know likes you. (Judgmental people are blind; they pretend they do not have the universal human nerve of guilt and shame; you feel worse!) . . . Forgiveness will flow as if transfused into the circuit of forgiveness created between the two of you.

"Our need to be forgiven feeds our capacity to forgive, and our capacity to forgive derives from our need to be forgiven . . ." Granting forgiveness and seeking it are two sides of a door to the same house . . . "the same key that gets you through one can help you through the other".

Well-presented and well-documented, this book contains excellent anecdotal information in clear, concise terms from a fresh perspective. Hallowell furnishes guidelines on the "how to" of personal forgiveness and articulates the actual dynamic, the process, of forgiving. To my knowledge, it is some of the best, most current and substantive information of its kind. Based on Hallowell's own experiences, this book has personal as well as practical relevance for professionals in the field.

3. Collective/Community Forgiveness: The Truth and Reconciliation Council (Apartheid Amnesty), South Africa, 2003.

The work of the Council was based on the idea that forgiveness is enabled through a reciprocal process. In empathy, a person reaches out to the other and says, "I can feel the pain you feel for having caused me pain." Then internal psychological dynamics will compel most of us toward forming an empathetic connection with another in pain.

In an external context, truth-telling for amnesty allows dialogue through the language of restoration, making reconciliation a possibility. Hope is where such transformation begins.

Nurturing conditions make forgiveness conceivable and possible, subject to the answers to two questions: having performed the unthinkable/atrocity, is the doer's authentic remorse achievable? And if expressed, is the remorse genuine? (It could be a cry for moral leniency.)

—Pumla Gobodo-Madikizela

4A. Forgiving the Unforgivable: The Story of Bud Welch (Murder Victims' Families for Reconciliation), St. Paul, Minnesota, 2004.

Mr. Welch is the father of a victim of the Oklahoma City bombing in 1995. Julie Marie, his only child, was 24 years old; her body was found three days after the blast. He describes his grief process as excruciating. He experienced outrage, alcoholism, reality shock, grieving, and finally the mourning of his daughter. His healing process began when he met Timothy McVeigh's father and sister. He identified with their pain, and during the trial and sentencing, they formed an empathic bond. Mr. Welch attended the execution with the McVeigh family and the parents of other victims.

To a person, these people all agreed that no sense of resolution or relief came with the man's execution. Forgiveness came to them over time, by using the energy from their anger to make the world a better place.

Bud Welch is currently a board member of Murder Victims' Families for Reconciliation.

—from a Minnesotans Against the Death Penalty Forum at Brady Educational Center, University of Saint Thomas, St. Paul, Minnesota, 2004

4B. Forgiving the Unforgivable: the Innocence Project, St. Paul, Minnesota, 2003.

The Innocence Project is the last court of appeal for the falsely accused and wrongly incarcerated. It was started in 1992 by attorneys Scheck and Neufeld at the Benjamin N. Cardoza School of Law in New York. While wrongful convictions are neither isolated nor rare, this project handles only cases where post-conviction DNA testing of evidence can yield conclusive proof of innocence. Students handle cases as a clinic while supervised by a team of attorneys and clinic staff.

Having gone nationwide, the Innocence Project was established in Minneapolis-St. Paul in 2000, housed at

Hamline Law School in St. Paul. The board chair of the Twin Cities organization, Attorney Edward Magarian, listed some of the project's major accomplishments to date: the prison system has become more supportive in nature, such as allowing prisoners to receive private mail for legal purposes; bipartisan support has been generated in the legislatures; and legal, educational and law enforcement groups have set common goals to work toward standardizing relevant procedures.

In the Twin Cities, The Innocence Project (for exonerees) has joined forces with Amicus (for ex-felons) to explore ways in which they might share mutually beneficial services and resources.

Suggested Ways to Address Personal Forgiveness Issues

The following examples of ways to address personal forgiveness issues suggest a kind of 'moral housekeeping' that enables us to harvest the meaning we give to our life's experiences:

- Daily journaling of past and present forgiveness issues (per Ira Pogeroff) as they come up
- A 'testimonial dinner' for several friends/mentors/relatives (used when seeking reconciliation in relationships)
- Composing and writing letters which remain unsent
- Dealing with grievances by expressing deep emotion (anger or grief), to gain closure and insight
- With a trusted other, communicating opinions or

controversial points of view in a safe, non-threatening atmosphere.

As Hargrave points out, one of the most powerful ways to address forgiveness is by the use of rituals and symbols. "Rituals are powerful because they combine our actions with specific meanings", especially when the action is distinct, out of our ordinary sphere, and its meaning is deeply important to us. A ritual might mean the burning of papers or burying of objects symbolic of the offense; a symbolic act of "penance" asked of and performed by the offender; praying for or together with the offender; and so on. Even the setting for the ritual may be significant. The possibilities are almost endless, unique to each situation. (See also Appendix B, The Act of Forgiving: A Ritual.)

Further assistance is available within most wisdom traditions for transforming hardness of the heart into compassion:

- Christian examples: Act of Contrition, Sacrament of Confession, The Lord's Prayer
- Jewish examples: High Holy Days—Day of Atonement; the Instrument of Self-Assessment used before the Day of Atonement (product of the Tikkun community, Rabbi Michael Lerner)
- Self-affirmations, both written and verbal
- Meditation and contemplation around life's transcendent issues, asking questions of the Universe, or a passionate inquiry born of an encounter with life and one's proximity to death.

My own study of the forgiveness process shows the following features to be essential:

- Over time, the elements of safe connection plus contact, whether formal or informal, tend to allow trust between the parties to develop

- A cohort professional person or group who is trustworthy, knowledgeable and can be respected creates the feeling of safety

- When others receive the seeker with unconditional acceptance, a nonjudgmental atmosphere is created. Unburdening the self can allow healing to begin, and active listening facilitates the process

- When a listener says something like, "I believe it happened the way you said it did," it validates the other's personhood

- A statement like "you have survived your own Auschwitz" acknowledges that one person has seen the pain of the other, and establishes an empathic connection.

Gerontological services specialists are therefore wise to create and convey permission, protection, perspective, and safe process. However, keep in mind that there may be times when the practitioner will be impotent to influence change, because the client or the circumstances have become unmanageable; or the desired outcome has been blocked by insurmountable obstacles.

CHAPTER ELEVEN

Gerotranscendence

"Many resilient older adults have survived multiple crises to accumulate compensatory wisdom and learn spiritual strength while they continue to grow developmentally."

"People who are resilient have the ability to move beyond being survivors
  to being thrivers . . ."

—from Ramsey & Blieszner

The Theory

Erik Erikson called the final stage of adult growth and development "ultimate maturity". Lars Tornstam named it "gerotranscendence", or, moving to a higher level of maturity to harvest wisdom—the task most paramount as people enter the last third of their existence on earth, elderhood.

An individual with this worldview experiences life as a personal, spiritual journey, with a sense of connectedness to the whole. In effectively dealing with tragic conditions over time, such an individual develops "spiritual resilience". Knowledge is not immunity from pain, yet nurturing strength of spirit through the pain can bring wisdom and grace.

Characteristics

Lars Tornstam, Ph.D., is a Professor of Social Gerontology, Institute of Social Medicine, at the University of Copenhagen, Denmark. The qualitative indicators of gerotranscendence he describes, as summarized below, are based on results from the Swedish Nurses' Study, which he conducted from 1999 to 2000.

An individual may exhibit one or several of the following signs of "enlightened maturity", which can be expressed as tasks, along with skills for completing them:

The Universal Dimension.

- To experience more connectedness between the past and the present, be open to your changing perspective on the meaning and/or value of time.
- To strengthen your connection with other generations, appreciate their legacy, e.g., by studying your genealogy, transmitting family stories, etc.
- To decrease fears around your own death, consider your legacy to those you will leave behind, doing what you can to ease their pain.
- To accept and appreciate the "mystery of life", hold the unexplainable lightly yet respectfully.
- To be open to the universal in the particular, expand your capacity to find joy in "the little things" that interest and delight you.

The Personal Dimension.

- To rediscover or redefine aspects of your self and your history, learn to re-evaluate realistically, without guilt, shame or blaming.

- To appreciate your true place in the human family, let go of the need to be the "star of the show", the "victim", or any other self-involved role; rather, become an authentic person.

- To become more self-confident and less approval-seeking, experience the "high" of altruistic acts, which become rewards in themselves.

- To reclaim your child within, be willing to revisit childhood scenes with the fresh understanding of the loving, forgiving parent, the knowing adult, who smiles kindly upon that innocent being.

- To realize and reframe the way your life's events—the puzzle—have formed a whole picture, be willing to arrange for periods of solitude and reflection, avoiding "busy-ness" for its own sake.

The social dimension.

- To cultivate and deepen your most meaningful relationships, become selective about how and with whom to spend your time, eliminating the superficial.

- To clarify the difference between your true self and the roles you have had to play in life, you may want to abandon old roles and try out new ones.

- To resurrect your sense of child-like freedom, now

seasoned with maturity, enjoy seeing through unnecessary, meaningless social norms and abandoning them—which Tornstam calls "emancipated innocence".

- To cultivate acceptance of life's ambiguities, let go of needing to judge "right vs. wrong" in self and others; avoid giving out unsolicited opinions and advice.

- To feel more connected to the spiritual plane and become less attached to the material, start to value the freedom of "less is more", and to appreciate beauty for its own sake, especially that found in nature.

If, level by level, over time, we can experience this spirit-based state of enlightenment—or gerotranscendence—we can enhance quality of life and spiritual well-being, not only for ourselves but also for all within our sphere.

Principal contributor: Anne Meissner, Ph.D.

CHAPTER TWELVE

The Value of Work

"Work gives meaning to life."
—Victor Frankl

"Things mean what we say they mean."
—the Author

Note: The material in this chapter, as in several others, is intended to address issues we may be facing both in our own professional lives and in the lives of our clients.

In our authentic maturity, it is important to understand "what we get from work" in addition to money. A partial list includes:

- A basis for personal identity
- A basis for our sense of worth in the world
- A way of structuring or spending time
- An arena for making friends and socializing
- A source of new experiences, creativity and self-expression
- A means to prestige and recognition
- An opportunity of be of service to others.

We live in a world where people are living longer and a great many are planning, for various reasons, to work longer. The traditional standard of using a certain age to decide when it is time to leave the job, or "retire", is fading. While a few enlightened companies are retaining valued older workers, more and more people are opting to leave their jobs early in order to reinvent, or "re-fire" (as in re-ignite) their careers and personal lives.

Official retirement, whether planned or sudden (e.g., forced by circumstance such as disability), can usher in multiple losses at multiple levels, including: the material, as in reduced income/lifestyle; the social, as in a smaller circle of friends; the psychological, experienced as disorientation, loss of identity, and diminished self-confidence. For some, the concurrent death of a partner or spouse may double the blow.

But eventually our natural human life-force will reassert itself, urging us to overcome our pain and "reach for the more", a process essential to regaining our sense of place in the world. Even if we need help to work through this cycle of grief, especially depression, the result will bring a greater sense of self and of mastery over our lives.

Life review and reassessment are key to our reorientation, as we ask: Who have I been, and who can I be now? My earlier life decisions had been influenced by roles and responsibilities, most of which no longer apply. What meaning can I take from how I have contributed in the past and apply that to the present? What skills and personal resources am I bringing with me? These and similar questions can usher in, or enhance, our next stage of adult development (see Chapter 11).

The benefits of this process, of harvesting meaning from who we have been and affirming who we want to become, are immeasurable. Through it, we can recover, reinvent, and recreate an authentic self. Courses, seminars, and audio and video resources abound to support us in our process of becoming. All we need do is reach out.

And by so doing, we reinforce the emerging social norm that becoming "older" need no longer be defined as the unavoidable decline of "getting old", and that, in fact, is supported by the recent—and very convincing—area of research called "brain fitness".

(See Appendix C, Brain Fitness, for a list of potential research applications.)

Part Four: Client Issues, Interpersonal

CHAPTER THIRTEEN

Families

Families and Group Dynamics

In today's world, the definition of "family group" covers a spectrum of combinations and permutations, e.g.: family of origin, of adoption, of choice, ad hoc, blended, etc.

Here, we are concerned with the degree to which the client and the client's "family group" all come together and work together with you and your team to resolve problems.

All relationship situations involving communication and decision-making—whether personal, professional, couple, or family—are dynamic, and these dynamics are impervious to material wealth, quality of life, or social status. A family unit, established over time, is a type of group. Each time a member is added, subtracted or repositioned in a role, there is a shift. Group dynamics operate, and group process applies.

This process determines the group's cohesiveness and its subsequent degree of effective functioning. To the degree that group members' talents and skills can interact freely and relationships, roles and the like remain appropriately balanced and respectful, levels of trust and intimacy can deepen. For some family groups, restrictions abound; such things will never happen.

As a professional doing your best work, counsel from the highest moral and ethical state you can maintain. Keep appropriate boundaries. *The Four Agreements* by Don Miguel Ruiz lists these guiding principles: "Be impeccable with your word; Don't take anything personally; Don't make assumptions;" and "Always do your best."

As far as you are able and without drawing attention to it, facilitate clear, crisp communication between the family group and the team, for however long they co-exist. Whenever possible, establish a spokesperson to represent each faction. At this point, deal in facts, not opinions; assessment, not evaluation; and maintain a high degree of privacy and confidentiality. Function as an informed observer, not forgetting that you come as a stranger to this group or groups.

Keep in mind that the entire situation has the potential to become dysfunctional. Facilitate, do not dictate. Set parameters; do not try to exercise control. Acknowledge and reference any discussions held and any leadership that may emerge.

Remember the dynamics of transference and countertransference:

Transference: Without knowing or calculating it, other people may project their unresolved issues and problems onto you as a nurturing parent figure.

Countertransference: You as the nurturing parent figure may, without intention, project your own unresolved issues and conflicted emotions into the situation.

As the case proceeds to its conclusion, varying degrees of intense emotion may surface and subside within the family and within the team; long-term issues from the past may trigger like emotions in the present.

Do not engage in any conflict. If necessary, ask for help and guidance, and replace yourself if and when appropriate. One possibility worth considering is to ask a colleague to "sit in." Just remember that new group members create new dynamics.

Keep in mind that anyone can begin a lawsuit against anyone for any reason, and everything that takes place is subject to perceptions and interpretations. As a professional in a professional setting, you are somewhat vulnerable. (The Federal Privacy Act is useful to know).

Attend to your own spiritual growth, personal care, and unresolved issues. Your own issues, especially if they are fresh, can trigger intense moments for you. Resolve these for your personal benefit later, outside the situation.

—based on the work of Emma Walsh, Ph.D., Chicago Institute of Health, presented at an MCDES* conference; revised, edited, and condensed by the Author with permission, 2003

Recognizing Denial

"Denial is a defensive process whereby painful thoughts and feelings associated with reality are unconsciously rejected or avoided."

—the Author

One of the strongest dysfunctional mechanisms that can damage family unity in a time of crisis is denial—denial by

*Minnesota Coalition for Death Education and Support

any of the parties, of any of the facts. Alertness to this process and recognizing its signs are essential for the caring professional, who can gently question and calm the sufferer, and refocus the group on the real crisis at hand.

Some denial is inevitable, at least in the initial phase of family participation when everyone, including the client, is struggling to accept the reality presenting itself. However, when members of the family cling to distorted perceptions, their persistent denial will undermine any effective decision-making about an appropriate response to the situation. The nurturing professional must gently assert the facts, and present a clear definition of the problem to be solved or the decision to be made.

The human instinct cleverly offers a variety of unique, observable behaviors—usually at the other-than-conscious level—that signal the manifestation of denial, and may be visible to a neutral party but remain invisible to the family or client. Signs of denial in progress may include any or several of the following.

Doing nothing, then justifying it with:

> Grandiosity—making the problem too big to solve
>
> Minimizing—making the problem too small to bother with
>
> Passivity—hoping someone else will take care of it.

Agitating, that is, doing something else instead of facing the problem:

> Body movements—like fidgeting, pacing, smoking, drinking
>
> Busywork—such as paperwork, cooking, cleaning—activities often rationalized as being necessary or useful.

Over-adapting:
> A direct attempt to avoid the painful reality and
> any responsibility for a resolution, such as a child-
> like dependency on the "experts" to fix it.

Incapacitation, whereby the person makes it obvious
that he or she is unable to cope—so someone else has
to do it—becoming:
> "Sick" (symptoms may be psychosomatic),
> immobilized, helpless
>
> "Stupid", claim lack of competence, unable to
> function, overwhelmed
>
> "Crazy", possibly to the point of a psychotic break
> with reality.

The skilled practitioner will, again, find it necessary to
calm and refocus the group, and restate the problem.

It is natural in an intensely emotional, loaded situation
to want to disown any involvement or to blame someone
else. Frequently, painful issues from the past will resurface.
In a crisis such as a death, especially if it is tragic or sudden,
denial will almost certainly be exhibited by one or more of
the survivors, and may be perceived as lack of cooperation
or worse, as opposition.

Case in point: when it comes to the funeral, often no
plan is in place and no funds have been set aside, setting
off even more conflict. In fact, dysfunction among the
planners is so common that one state, New York, has
recently passed a law requiring that the group choose one
spokesperson, a "primary mourner", to work with the
funeral director, and if he or she does not, the director may
secure a court order to appoint one.

Professionals dealing with clients who are in resistance mode may want to consult William Glasser's classic *Reality Therapy*, based on his conclusions regarding avoidance behaviors (denial, repression, and suppression).

CHAPTER FOURTEEN

Types of Marriages

"The sum of the parts is greater than the whole."
—from Gestalt theory

As noted in the previous chapter, today's "core families" vary considerably in makeup and the unique system of interactions and relationships they establish. A married or committed couple forms the basic system, and the *quality* of their marriage relationship affects interactions within the core family.

In a crisis situation, even with emotions ranging from benumbed denial to unbearable pain and not functioning at their best, a couple will still bring that quality to the table. Learning how to assess their relationship—without judging it, them, or their behavior—is paramount for the professional. And it bears repeating: do not allow yourself to be pulled into any pre-existing or emerging conflict; keep your focus on managing the case.

One example of an assessment tool is this survey, conducted and presented at a workshop by David H. L. Olson, Ph.D., author and co-author of numerous books on marriage and the family. In this sample, the qualities of the marriage relationship were reported by the couples themselves. (You may know other methods and criteria.)

Type 1. Highly vitalized:
—Feel highly satisfied in almost all dimensions of their lives and relationship
—Get along well
—Are personally well-integrated
—Have strong internal resources
—Agree on most external resources
—Resolve difficulties
—Feel economically 'better off'
—Are in first marriage, Caucasian, Protestant, and come from intact families

Type 2. Harmonious:
—Include all of the items under Type 1
—Experience parenting as a source of distress, self-centered children as a burden

Type 3. Balanced:
—Feel moderately satisfied
—Consider communication and problem-solving to be their strengths

Type 4. Traditional:
—Are relatively stable
—Feel moderately satisfied with many elements of the relationship
—Find satisfaction from outside sources such as religion, friends, and extended family

Type 5. Conflicted:
—Feel dissatisfied with many facets of the relationship
—Avoid issues or fail to settle them

—Focus on and gain satisfaction from outside experiences

Type 6. Financially focused:
—Put career first
—Engage in conflict, with bitter personal attacks
—Are held together by money

Type 7. Devitalized:
—Have a highly unstable marriage
—Feel pervasive unhappiness with all aspects of the relationship.

In your assessment, pay particular attention to signs of inconsistencies, such as making then breaking agreements; or of incongruence, as in a disconnect between expressed emotion and body language (smiling when angry).

Mixed messages erode trust and impede the process. Your understanding of the dynamics at play will facilitate it.

CHAPTER FIFTEEN

Multiple Identities and Their Impact

"Ethnicity is a social reality that will require the professional to be more culturally competent. Race, gender, religion, class, immigration status, age, sexual orientation and disability are the other critical identity issues that we must consider in order to understand our clients."

—from McGoldrick, at al

Each human enters this world with a spirit (life energy connected to the cosmic web), free will, intellect, and more. While it is our job individually as humans to make our lives work, we are given the set of determinants we arrive with and the certainty that we will leave. In between, the context in which these determinants exist will influence our behavioral decisions, as will any trauma, disease, disability, etc. that we may encounter along the way.

Just as multiple intelligences exist, multiple identities exist and influence our behavioral decision-making. As noted above, these influences may include our cultural, ethnic, and religious background as well the individual identity we develop as we grow through life's experiences.

The kind of counseling and support we as professionals can deliver will be influenced by the norms and values adopted by the individuals and groups we serve, in situations of crisis, trauma, poor health, and even death. The relationship built between the practitioner and the designated "client" is primary, but situational outcomes will also be influenced by the client's own ethnic, cultural, religious, and family affiliations.

To wit, here is just a partial list of the multitude of factors—values, beliefs, norms and mores of the client and/or client group—which can affect outcomes:

How is the pain/trauma/crisis, be it physical or emotional, experienced? What is labeled as a problem or symptom? How is this communicated? What do they believe is the cause, the reason for this experience?

What is their attitude toward seeking help (is it okay) and toward the helping professions? What treatments or solutions do they desire or expect? Are they accepting of prescribed therapies, medications or alternatives?

How verbal or nonverbal are they? How optimistic or pessimistic? Do they feel able to cope? Do they seem vulnerable and dependent, or strong and independent, or stubbornly counterdependent? Is pride a factor?

Is there a wisdom tradition that influences this person or group? Does this group have/give permission to mourn when appropriate?

Are boundaries an issue? Within highly emotional families or unstable groups, it may be difficult to determine whom to address and/or with whom to negotiate. (See Chapter 5 on the Use and Abuse of Power.)

Recognizing the limitations of what is possible may require, for instance, assembling a multiple-approach team to deal with all the issues involved, or even removing one's self from a particular client or case. In any event, we must create a safe environment in which such decisions can be made and, whenever possible, for resolution to emerge.

EPILOGUE

"To finish is a sadness to a writer—a little death".
—John Steinbeck

Working on this project, I am now remembering what I have learned before: that when you actualize a goal, you also suffer a loss. I find that I cannot let go of the creative phase of writing this book without addressing its ending. But from here, it also appears that every ending is a new beginning, and everything is a transition, a bridge, to another phase.

According to one currently accepted view of adult development, I am in my "second adulthood", which comprises two stages: from age 45 to 65, mastery; and from age 65 to 85, integrity. The National Council on Aging offers a parallel view: age 65 to 75 is "young-old"; age 75 to 85 is "middle old"; and beyond age 85 is "old-old". All of which makes me a young-old person transitioning into the next phase of my development. What will that phase look like?

As "Wave 2010" approaches, the "baby boomer generation" streams into the increasing flow of people who are living longer, working longer, and retiring later. Some are, or will become, the "sandwich generation", struggling to provide for children as well as care for aging parents.

Available services are, at present, glaringly inadequate, and clearly require updating as well as streamlining. Quality-of-life issues that must be addressed will include: greater emphasis on maintaining health and wellness; more choices for in-home medical and non-medical support services; plus mobility, transportation, and accessibility—especially in rural areas. So much work needs to be done, where to begin?

These phase and work questions have dovetailed for me: I was recently appointed by Governor Pawlenty to the Minnesota Board on Aging, where I will be serving as co-chair on the Public Policy Committee. There, I can help to initiate and facilitate addressing some of the issues described above.

It may appear to be a happy coincidence that all of my life and professional experiences up until now lead to this work, this phase, but I do not think so: I was *intentional!*

May you be as fortunate.

Give, and it shall be given unto you"
Is still the truth about life.
But giving life is not so easy.
It doesn't mean handing it out to some mean fool,
Or letting the living dead eat you up.
It means kindling the life-quality where it was not,
Even if it's only in the whiteness
Of a washed pocket handkerchief.

Part Five: Appendices

Potential Legal Issues for Senior Citizens*

Age Discrimination
Contract Disputes
Creditor Harassment
High-pressure Door-to-Door or Telemarketing Sales
Energy Assistance
Family Problems
Health Care Problems
Home Repairs
Landlord/Tenant Problems
Living Wills
Medicare and Medical Assistance
Medigap Insurance, HMO Policies
Nursing Home Situations
Patients' Rights
Pension Plans
Planning for Incapacity
Power of Attorney, Advance Care Directive
Private Housing/Public Housing
Social Security
Social Services
Supplemental Security Income (SSI)
Unemployment Compensation
Unfair Sales Practices

Veterans' Benefits
Warranty Enforcement

—from the Senior Citizens' Law Project,
Minnesota Board on Aging

*excluding criminal matters

APPENDIX B

The Act of Forgiving: A Ritual

Leader issues invitation:

Please join me in creating a sacred space. Close your eyes; take silence; sit comfortably; breathe deeply. Visualize this group and this place bathed in an opalescent cloud of brilliant white light.

[Bell rings]

Leader reads:

Forgiveness is an *attitude* of the spirit, a *decision* of the mind and heart, and a *process* that unfolds once we achieve the attitude and make the decision.

We must recognize forgiveness of self or others as a necessary, intentional andgenuine act of free will. Lack of forgiveness is poison for the human spirit.

Over time, the lack of forgiveness emerges as an obstacle to our present"beingness."

As the issues involved come to light, this reality is clear: we cannot move on until we let go of whatever obstacle is binding us to the past.

[Lighting of candle]

Leader continues:
This light is a symbol of our energy and our burning desire for wholeness.

[Bell rings]

Leader continues:
We now choose as an act of free will to journey "as pilgrim": to move through the process —- of Recognition, Reflection, Release, and Reorientation.

[Silent pause]

Leader:
Let us begin.

[Bell rings]

Group in unison—Recognition:
I have a blister on my heart.
It is a place of unforgiveness.
I long for healing and for wholeness.

[Silent pause]

Group continues:
I have a wound upon my heart.
I am not this wound—I am more!

*I now align my will with the divine will of the Universe.
I ask for transformation of this energy to be released as
good in the world.*

[Silent pause]
[Bell rings]

Group in unison—Reflection:
*A burden on my heart eats at my integrity,
keeps me ever weary, ever sad.
It gnaws at my peace.*

*My walking forward is weakened.
I am distorted by my suffering and my hurt.
My vision is marred.*

[Silent pause]
[Bell rings]

Leader—Release:
Please join me in this symbolic ritual of release.

[Special paper is passed to each group member,
with pencil]

[Candle (still lit) is joined by a container of water]

Leader:
Record a word or symbol representing your
forgiveness issue on a sheet of paper. (Use as many as
you need.) This water represents symbolic cleansing

and soothing comfort. When you are ready, each of you is invited to step forward and place your paper in the water. Just as the water dissolves the paper, your intention will dissolve your wound.

[Participants each place paper(s) in container of water]

[Silent pause]
[Bell rings]

Group in unison—Reorientation:
We will do what we must do to continue letting go.

Leader:
Know that while moving on may happen slowly, you *will* come home to yourself. A quiet resurrection will take place, in each of us.

Group:
The desire for release, healing and wholeness has arisen in us all.
We are changed.

Leader and group:
Thank you, Universal Light.
So be it.

[Silent pause]
[Bell rings]

Leader—Option One:

To complete and to celebrate this ritual, we will close by singing the Quaker   hymn "Simple Gifts", to the melody of Aaron Copeland's "Appalachian Spring".

(Go to next page for words.)

Leader—Option Two:

To close this ritual, we will exit in gratitude and silence. Bless you all.

[Candle is extinguished]
[Bell rings]

Leader—Option One, continued:

'Tis a gift to be simple,
'Tis a gift to be free,
'Tis a gift to come down
Where we ought to be.
And when we find ourselves/ in a place just right
We'll be in a valley/ of love and delight.
When true simplicity is gained,
To bow and to bend,
We will not be ashamed
To turn, to turn
'Twill be our delight,
'Til by turning, turning,
We come 'round right

To close this ritual, we will exit in gratitude and silence.
Bless you all.

[Candle is extinguished]
[Bell rings]

—Written and first presented by Carol Lee Bratter
in Minneapolis, MN, 2004

Brain Fitness/
Research Applications

Brain fitness vs. brain aging

Preventing the irreversible loss of brain tissue

The graying of America—consequences for brain health

The true age of a brain— the brain and the immune system

Modern theories of brain decline—structural damage, free radicals, nutritional deficiencies, lifetime risk of Alzheimer's disease, etc.

Brain aging and common conditions—depression, hypothyroidism, B-12 deficiency, autoimmune disease, circulatory pathology, oral disease, etc.

Effects of medications—interference with brain fitness, memory, cognition

Forgetfulness—normal difficulties with language, fatigue, sleep, spatial disorientation, as distinct from Alzheimer's/true dementia

Starving for perfection—low-calorie diets, caloric restriction, insulin resistance

Brain consequences of high-calorie/high fat diets—of overweight, obesity, diabetes

Eating meat and brain health—Mad Cow disease, Alzheimer's

Eating fish and brain health—Omega-3 fatty acids, dyslexia, ADHD; mercury and other toxins

Language – fumbling for words, "left brain" vs. "right brain", word games

The brain as computer—the principle of "use it or lose it"

Measurements of brain fitness—memory and intellect, language and function, etc.; interpreting test results

Can "brain fitness" be increased?—crossword puzzles, Sudoku, Rubik's cube, etc.

Recollection exercises—mnemonic devices, strategies for 'retracing' memories

Brain fitness and emotions—hormones, effects of the stress/pleasure responses

Problem-solving—leisure-time activities for a positive effect on brain fitness

Video gaming—the surge of popularity among mature populations

Computer software for brain fitness—choosing, using, side effects.

—based on the seminar "Brain Fitness After 30", given by Laura Pawlak, Ph.D., M.S., in St. Paul, MN, 2007

APPENDIX D

Caregiver Facts

Caregiving Categories (not necessarily sequential):

- Preventive
- Anticipatory
- Supervisory
- Instrumental (the most common)
- Protective (the most difficult).

Caregiver Population:

- Most commonly, the primary caregiver is a partner, relative or close friend.
- The largest group of caregivers is female, usually a wife, often a daughter-in-law.
- Women caregivers outnumber men by a ratio of three to one.
- Wives care for husbands more frequently than husbands care for wives.
- Adult children often supplement the amount of assistance needed, taking on additional financial, social and emotional burdens.

- Adult children often step in to replace a deceased caregiver spouse.

- *"Family caregiver help is the most significant factor in reducing the cost of medical care."*

—from their position statement on
"Family Caregiving in Minnesota",
by the Minnesota Metropolitan Council, 2007

The Thanatology Association has recently released a report with a troubling conclusion: *"Caregiver mortality is significantly on the rise."*

Frequently, the primary caregiver provides care in spite of, rather than because of, the past relationship. Care of self (and other loved ones) may begin to suffer from neglect.

At greatest risk is the adult female child, who may have feelings of guilt, frustration, resentment and anger (there are more). Further, no matter how much love the child feels, or how responsible, strain will develop—especially if the care is intensive and protracted.

How the primary caregiver perceives the burden, positively or negatively, will determine the potential for the elder abuse and/or caregiver mortality. In circumstances where negative emotion builds up, elder abuse is more likely to develop. When the caregiver's stress load brings on low morale, depression or burnout, mortality is more likely to result.

A Note to Professionals
Who May Become Caregivers

I have added the following as the result of witnessing a recent event.

If the decision whether or not to step in as caregiver falls to you, assess all the facts of the situation in order to make an informed decision. (See Appendix E, Potential Challenges Facing Caregivers.) Take into account what you know about yourself, and be honest.

As stated earlier, knowledge is not necessarily immunity; it is a good beginning. However, if you become a caregiver for a loved one, there will be times when all of your talent and experience will not save you from needing help yourself. Do not wait for a crisis as an excuse to reach out! Give yourself permission to rest, process what you are experiencing, and regain perspective; protect yourself from burnout. (See Appendix F, A Caregiver's Bill of Rights.)

Also important for both/all of you if death is on the horizon: pay special attention beforehand to what the survivor(s) will need to know: where relevant papers are kept; whether funeral arrangements have been specified; and so on. I have seen too many people left to deal with a helpless mess, requiring endless sorting, paperwork, and long lists of necessary calls to make—all at a time when grieving should be their only priority.

So first, take care of yourself.

Caregiver Challenges

- Survival Checklist: what you need to know
- Coping with Crisis: facing the realities; getting things under control
- Emotional Issues: sorting out the real problems
- Family Issues: problems; getting relatives to work together; long-distance care
- Financial Crisis: getting finances in order; dealing with poverty
- Health Issues: how aging affects the body; dealing with illness or injury; promoting wellness
- Alzheimer's Disease: warning signs; what to do
- Housing Issues: home health care vs. moving to a care facility; choosing the facility
- Medical Assistance: community resources
- Medicare/Medigap Insurance: how does it work, what does it cover/cost, etc.
- Nursing home or Long-Term Care Insurance: is it wise, is it feasible
- The Impaired Person's Independence: what are the risks/benefits

- Driving Privileges: effects of aging on drivers; is it time to stop
- When a Parent Refuses to Cooperate: what to do
- Death and Dying: making preparations; what survivors will need to know
- Ombudsmen/Advocates for Seniors
- The Guilt and Anger Trap: breaking out
- Caregivers' Dilemma: how to help without burning out (see Appendix F).

—based on *Checklist for Aging, A Workbook for Care Giving*, by Warren Wolfe, originally published as columns in the *Minneapolis Star & Tribune*, 1992

A Caregiver's Bill of Rights

As a Caregiver, I have the right:

- To take care of myself. This is not an act of selfishness. It will enable me to take better care of my loved one.

- To seek help from others even though my loved one may object. I recognize the limits of my own endurance and strength.

- To maintain facets of my own life that do not include the person I care for, just as I would if he or she were healthy. I know that I do everything that I reasonably can for this person, and I have the right to do some things for myself.

- To get angry, be depressed and express other difficult emotions I may be feeling from time to time.

- To reject any attempt by my loved one (conscious or unconscious) to manipulate me through guilt, anger or depression.

- To receive consideration, affection, forgiveness and acceptance from my loved one for what I do, as long as I offer these in return.

- To take pride in what I am accomplishing, and to applaud the courage it sometimes takes to meet the needs of my loved one.

- To protect my individuality and my right to make a life for myself that will sustain me in the time when my loved one no longer needs my time and my help.

- To expect and demand that, as new strides are made in finding resources to aid impaired persons, similar strides will be made toward aiding and supporting caregivers as well.

—from the AHA magazine *Stroke Connection*,
Vol. 17, No. 6, 1995

BIBLIOGRAPHY

Articles, Lectures and Papers

Carlsson, Marianne, Ph.D., and Wadensten, Barbro, R.N., M.Sc. "Theory-driven Guidelines for Practical Care of Older People, Based on the Theory of Gerotranscendence." *Issues and Innovations in Nursing Practice*, Blackwell Publishing Ltd., 2003, pp. 462–470.

Carlsson, Marianne, Ph.D., and Wadensten, Barbro, R.N., M.Sc. "Signs of Gerotranscendence, Nursing Theory and Concept Development of Analysis." *Journal of Advanced Nursing*, Blackwell Science Ltd., 2001, pp. 635–642.

Frankl, Viktor, and Gerkin, Charles. "A Dialogue between Viktor Frankl and Charles Gerkin Regarding the Living Human Document and the Search for and the Will to Meaning." Luther Seminary Continuing Education Seminar, 2002.

Gustafson, Mona. "Forgiveness Issues and Process." Personal and Community Resources class lecture at Colonial Church of Edina, September 1999.

Kimble, Melvin A., Ph.D. "Gerontological Pastoral Caregiving, a Logotherapy Pastoral Perspective." From notes on a presentation by Dr. Kimble at Luther Seminary, 2002.

Robesson, James. "Research Project on Forgiveness Seeks Volunteers." Stanford Education Department Internet Newsletter. Online, January 6, 1999.

Reference Works

Chambers, Oswald. *Daily Readings from My Utmost for His Highest*. Nashville: T. Nelson Publishers, 1993.

Friedman, Dayle A., ed. *Jewish Pastoral Care, a Practical Handbook from Traditional and Contemporary Sources*. Woodstock, VT: Jewish Lights Publishing, 2001.

Hunter, Rodney J., ed. *Dictionary of Pastoral Care and Counseling*. Nashville: Abingdon Press, 1990.

Kimble, Melvin A., et al, eds. *Aging, Spirituality and Religion, a Handbook, Vols. 1 and 2*. Minneapolis: Augsburg Fortress Press, 1995 and 2003.

Maddox, George L., ed. *The Encyclopedia of Aging, a Comprehensive Resource in Gerontology and Geriatrics*. 2nd Ed. New York: Springer Publishing, 1995.

McGoldrick, Giordano and Pearce, eds. *Ethnicity and Family Therapy.* New York: Guilford Press, 1996.

Strong, Kohlenberger & Swanson. *The Strongest Strong's Exhaustive Concordance of the Bible, 21st Century Edition.* Grand Rapids, MI: Zondervan, 2001.

Tobin, Ellor and Anderson-Ray, eds. *Enabling the Elderly: Religious Institutions within the Community Service System.* Albany: State University of New York Press, 1986.

Thinline Bible, New International Version. Grand Rapids, MI: Zondervan, 1996.

Truth and Reconciliation Project Broadcast. Minneapolis: Minnesota Public Radio, January, 2004.

Books

Assagioli, Roberto, M.D. *The Act of Will.* New York: Viking Press, 1973.

Bragdon, Allen D. & Gamon, David. *Brains That Work a Little Bit Differently: Recent Discoveries about Common Mental Diversities.* South Yarmouth, MA: Brainwaves Books, 2000.

Csikszentmihalyi, Mihaly. *Flow: the Psychology of Optimal Experience.* New York: Harper & Row, 1990.

Erikson, Erik, with Joan Erikson and Helen Kivnick. *Vital Involvement in Old Age: the Experience of Aging in Our Time.* New York: Norton, 1986.

Fox, Matthew. *Sins of the Spirit, Blessings of the Flesh.* New York: Harmony Books, 1999.

Frankl, Victor E. *Man's Search for Meaning: an Introduction to Logotherapy.* 3rd Ed. New York: Simon & Schuster, 1984.

Glasser, William, M.D. *Reality Therapy, a New Approach to Psychiatry.* New York: Harper & Row, 1965.

Gobodo-Madikizela, Pumla. *A Human Being Died That Night: a South African Story of Forgiveness.* Boston: Houghton Mifflin, 2003.

Hallowell, Edward M., M.D. *Dare to Forgive.* Deerfield Beach, FL: Health Communications, 2004.

Hargrave, Terry, Ph.D. *Forgiving the Devil: Coming to Terms with Damaged Relationships.* Phoenix: Zeig, Tucker & Theisen, Inc., 2001.

Kimble, Melvin A., ed. *Frankl's Contribution to Spirituality and Aging.* New York: Haworth Pastoral Press, 2000.

Kohlberg, Lawrence. *The Psychology of Moral Development: the Nature and Validity of Moral Stages.* San Francisco: Harper & Row, 1984.

Luskin, Fred, M.D. *Forgiveness for Good: a Proven Prescription for Health and Happiness.* San Francisco: Harper San Francisco, 2002.

Mayeroff, Milton. *On Caring.* New York: Harper & Row, 1971.

Palmer, Parker J. *Let Your Life Speak: Listening for the Voice of Vocation.* San Francisco: Jossey-Bass, 2000.

Peck, M. Scott, M.D. *The Road Less Traveled: a New Psychology of Love, Traditional Values and Spiritual Growth.* New York: Simon & Schuster, 1978.

Ramsey, Janet L. & Blieszner, Rosemary. *Spiritual Resiliency in Older Women: Models of Strength for Challenges through the Life Span.* Thousand Oaks, CA: Sage Publications, 1999.

Ramshaw, Elaine. *Ritual & Pastoral Care.* Philadelphia, Fortress Press, 1987.

Ruiz, Don Miguel. *The Four Agreements: A Practical Guide to Personal Freedom.* San Rafael, CA: Amber-Allen, 1995.

Schachter-Shalomi, Zalman, and Miller, Ronald S. *From Age-ing to Sage-ing: a Profound New Vision of Growing Older.* New York: Warner Books, 1997.

Thompson, C. Michael. *The Congruent Life: Following the Inward path to Fulfilling Work and Inspired Leadership*. San Francisco: Jossey-Bass, 2000.

Tolle, Eckhart. *The Power of Now, a Guide to Spiritual Enlightenment*. Novato, CA: New World Library, 1999.

Tornstam, Lars, Ph.D. *Gerotranscendence: a Developmental Theory of Positive Aging*. New York: Springer Publishing, 2005.

Viorst, Judith. *Necessary Losses*. New York: Simon & Schuster, 1986.

Wilkinson, James A. *A Family Caregivers Guide to Planning and Decision Making for the Elderly*. Minneapolis: Fairview Press, 1999.

Other Resources

www.aarp.org
AARP's comprehensive resource covering numerous aspects of older adulthood, with links to a long list of related websites, e.g., regarding health, legislation, insurance, quality-of-life, and so forth. Membership confers benefits not available elsewhere.

www.agingwithdignity.org
> For "Five Wishes", an excellent fill-in booklet for communicating wishes to family/caregivers in case of serious illness. In certain states, can serve as living will and/or durable power of attorney for health care.

www.fortisfamily.com
> For "Your Planning Guide", a thorough yet simple fill-in workbook for survivors to consult at the time of a death, including funeral instructions, location of important papers, etc. An appropriate accompaniment to legal and spiritual wills.

www.nia.nih.gov
> Leads to a searchable database of 250+ national health organizations that provide help to older persons. One example: www.eldercare.gov, a national eldercare community services locator. The initials NIA refer to the National Institute on Aging, "leading the federal effort on aging research".

www.ethicalwill.com and *www.yourlivingwill.com*
> Dr. Barry Baines and Susan Turnbull each guide us through their respective processes for creating a spiritual, or ethical, will—a non-material legacy. Useful as a tool for "harvesting" the value and meaning of one's life.

www.aoa.gov
> Administration on Aging

www.cms.gov
   Centers for Medicare & Medicaid Services

www.cyberseniors.org
   Cyber Seniors

www.elderhostel.org
   Elderhostel

www.fda.gov
   Food and Drug Administration

www.fbi.gov
   Federal Bureau of Investigation

www.healthfinder.gov
   Healthfinder

www.pensionrights.org
   Pension Rights Center

www.seniors-site.com
   Senior Sites

www.seniorsearch.com
   Senior Search

www.senior.org
   Seniors Coalition

www.seniorscorps.org
    Seniors Corps

www.ssa.gov
    Social Security Administration

www.bva.va.gov
    Veterans Benefits Administration

www.whitehouse.gov
    The White House

Note: While authors and publishers cited may host their own websites, all resources are subject to change at any time.—Ed.

About the Author

Carol Lee Bratter's background in career development, human resources, and the multiple issues facing our aging population is extensive.

She began her habit of lifelong learning at a young age, going in a few short years from job placement trainee to managing a branch office in Minneapolis. She eventually opened her own successful employment/career development agency in 1974. By applying her learnings from human relations training, Carol began to reinvent the way her company did business; while continuing as avid student as well as trainer/motivator, she became a pioneer in incorporating human services concepts into the workaday world.

The time came, however, when Carol faced the inevitable clash between serving the business's bottom line and continuing to grow as a person of integrity, an "Intentional Professional". In 1990, she closed her agency and embarked on a series of personal missions that more fully expressed the desire to employ her store of knowledge, talents and skills in the service of others.

Over the past several years, Carol has undergone intensive training in multiple interrelated disciplines, e.g., adult development, death and dying, lay chaplaincy for the elderly, and more.

Currently, Ms. Bratter continues her successful private practice as a Life Transitions Coach "for older professionals facing personal and/or professional life challenges." She belongs to several professional associations, has served on numerous boards, and was recently appointed by the Governor for a four-year term on the Minnesota Board on Aging, where she serves on the Public Policy Committee.

For further information, access Carol's website at www.carolbratter.com.

A Note from the Editor

Ever since our first project together in the 1970s, I have felt fortunate to collaborate with a woman as brilliant and gifted as Carol Bratter.

Her store of knowledge on the material herein is prodigious, and the words fairly fly onto the page from her amazing memory. (At times it is all I can do to keep up.)

It has been my challenge, and my honor, to ensure that her words and ideas coalesce into a manuscript that conveys exactly what she wants it to.

You, the Reader, are the beneficiary of a genuine gift. Use it well.

—M. K. Bryant

Journal Notes